ONE WORLD, MANY RELIGIONS

ONE WORLD, MANY RELIGIONS

THE WAYS WE WORSHIP

BY MARY POPE OSBORNE

ALFRED A. KNOPF
NEW YORK

To William Peck and Ruel Tyson,
wonderful teachers who made the world wider for me

ACKNOWLEDGMENTS:
This book would not have been possible without the help of
Adrienne Aurichio, Simon Boughton, Denise Cronin, Pastor Gregory P. Fryer,
Suzanne Glazer, Mina Greenstein, Dr. Ann Hoffman, Regina Kahney, Ruth
Katcher, Ed Miller, Beverly Moon, Dr. Mohammad Salem-Agwa,
and Rabbi Stephen J. Weissman.

Library of Congress Cataloging-in-Publication Data

Osborne, Mary Pope.
One world, many religions: the ways we worship / by Mary Pope Osborne.
p. cm.
Includes bibliographical references and index.
Summary: An illustrated introduction to comparative religion, discussing Judaism, Christianity, Islam,
Hinduism, Buddhism, Confucianism, and Taoism.
I. Religions—Juvenile literature. [I. Religions.] I. Title.
BL92.083 1996
291—dc20 96-836

ISBN 0-679-83930-5 (trade)
0-679-93930-X (lib. bdg.)

Printed in Singapore

10 9 8 7 6 5 4 3 2 1

First Edition

Picture credits follow the Index.

Title page: The Ishak Pasha palace and mosque,
on the border between Iran and Turkey.

CONTENTS

INTRODUCTION

How did the world begin? What is the purpose of life? What happens after we die?

Since the beginning of time, people have asked these questions. In their search for answers, they have often felt the presence of a sacred power, or powers.

The earliest people felt such powers in the sun, the moon, and the stars. They believed that sacred spirits lived in animals and beautiful places in nature.

Early people constantly turned to these powers for help. They prayed to the spirit of the bear for a good hunt and to Mother Earth for a good harvest. They offered thanks to the sun by singing and dancing.

Worship of the sacred was not something separate from daily life—it was life itself. It was woven through every activity, every dream and story. These ways of worship were the first religious practices.

The word *religion* comes from the Latin word *religare*, which means "to tie." Every time people worship, they are tied to the sacred. Their religion also ties them to one another, for it gives them a sense of community and purpose.

Today, many people around the world still practice ways of worship from ancient times. Tribal African religions, for instance, teach that after people die, their spirits continue to participate in the daily lives of their relatives and friends. For this reason, people often pray to the spirits of their dead loved ones, asking for rain, for abundant crops, and for healthy children.

Traditional Native American religions teach that the world is alive with the spirits of animals and forces of nature, such as Coyote, Raven, the great Sky Father, and the Earth Mother. Young Native Americans sometimes seek a vision from the spirit world to help them find their own special gifts and talents.

Followers of the Japanese Shinto religion believe that sacred forces inhabit the most beautiful places in nature, so they worship beside a waterfall, for example, or an old gnarled tree.

These religions, among others, keep some of the earliest traditions alive, and

◀ YOUNG DRUMMERS AT A SHINTO FESTIVAL IN JAPAN.

SHAMAN WOMEN IN SWAZILAND (AFRICA). SHAMANS ARE RELIGIOUS LEADERS WHO CONDUCT CEREMONIES TO HONOR THE SPIRITS OF THE DEAD. THEY ALSO HEAL THE SICK AND PREDICT THE FUTURE. THESE SHAMANS SHAKE NUTS INTO A PATTERN, THEN READ THE MESSAGE IN THE PATTERN TO FORESEE THE FUTURE.

when we learn about them—or practice them—we feel a deeper tie to the earth and the universe.

The earliest religions were passed from parents to children by word of mouth. None of their wisdom or stories were written down, because writing had not been invented. For this reason, we can never be certain about the exact origins and development of their teachings and practices.

Because of the invention of writing, however, we know a great deal about seven religions that began in the Middle East and Asia. One of these was Judaism, which began between three and four thousand years ago. Christianity eventually grew out of Judaism. Then the religion of Islam grew out of Judaism and Christianity.

At the same time that Jewish teachings were being written down in the Middle East, priests in India were recording the teachings of Hinduism. About 2,500 years ago, the writings of Buddhism grew out of Hinduism. Around the same time, scholars in China began writing down the teachings of Confucianism and Taoism.

Today, most religious people in the world practice one of these seven religions. All have had a deep effect on the laws and customs of the countries in which they are practiced. They have shaped art, literature, music, and education. They have determined the way people mark the passage of time. They have influenced the way parents raise their children. They have given the world magnificent stories, songs, buildings, holy objects, ceremonies, and festivals.

Although these seven religions have different beliefs and teach different ways to worship, they have certain important things in common:

They all seek to bring comfort to their followers.

They all offer thanks for the world's great beauty and goodness.

They all express awe and humility before the mysteries of the universe.

In this sense, they are all wise and enduring.

THIS YOUNG APACHE GIRL HAS BEEN SPRINKLED WITH YELLOW CATTAIL POLLEN—A SYMBOL OF FERTILITY—IN A CEREMONY MARKING HER PASSAGE FROM CHILDHOOD TO ADULTHOOD.

JUDAISM

The story of Judaism begins with a shepherd named Abraham and his wife, Sarah. They lived almost four thousand years ago in the ancient land of Ur, in what is now Iraq. At that time, the people of Ur worshiped many gods, including gods of fire, water, and the sky.

According to a Jewish legend, Abraham began to wonder which of these gods was the one true God. One day, when the sun was shining, Abraham decided the sun must be God. When the sun went down and the moon rose in the sky, he decided the moon was God. But when the moon vanished the next morning, Abraham decided there must be a power even greater than the sun or the moon—greater than all living things. He thought this great invisible power must be the one true God.

In time, this one true God spoke to Abraham and made a covenant, or agreement, with him. God promised to bless Abraham and Sarah and lead them to a far-

◄ A YOUNG JEWISH GIRL LIGHTS CANDLES FOR THE WEEKLY SABBATH, THE MOST SACRED JEWISH HOLIDAY. THE SABBATH BEGINS AT SUNDOWN ON FRIDAY AND ENDS AT NIGHTFALL ON SATURDAY.

away land called Canaan. In return, Abraham promised that he and his family would always be faithful to God.

From then on, Abraham and his descendants believed in only one God, a God who enters every human life in a personal way. This was a stunning new idea—one that made Judaism different from all other religions of the time.

After Abraham and Sarah reached Canaan, their son Isaac had a son named Jacob, who would later be called Israel. As the centuries passed, Abraham's descendants came to be called the Israelites. The Israelites eventually left Canaan because of a shortage of food. About five hundred years after Abraham's death, they were living in Egypt. At first the Egyptians treated them well, but the Israelites grew too numerous, and the Egyptian ruler forced them into slavery.

According to Jewish history, one day God spoke to an Israelite named Moses. God told Moses that he should lead the Israelites out of Egypt and back to the "Promised Land" of Canaan—the land God had promised to Abraham long ago.

Moses went to the Egyptian king and asked him to free the Israelite slaves. When the king said no, God caused ten terrible plagues to happen to the Egyptians, including a hailstorm, an infestation of locusts, and, worst of all, the death of every firstborn son. Finally, the king begged Moses to lead his people away.

The Israelites began to leave Egypt. But the king changed his mind and sent his soldiers after them to bring them back. The soldiers caught up with the Israelites at the Red Sea. The Israelites were trapped—water in front of them, soldiers behind.

Moses climbed up on a rock and prayed to God for help. Then he stretched his hand over the waters, and they parted. The Israelites crossed safely to the other side, and the waters returned, drowning the soldiers. At last, the Israelites were free from slavery. For the next forty years, they wandered in the desert, learning how to be a free people under the leadership of Moses and God.

During that time, God gave ten laws to Moses to give to the Israelites. These laws, called the Ten Commandments, were carved on stone tablets. They told the Israelites how they should behave in their daily lives.

Moses died before his people reached the Promised Land. But after his death, the Israelites carried the stone tablets bearing the Ten Commandments into Canaan. And there they built a great nation.

The Ten Commandments became the core of Judaism's holy book, which the Jews call the *Tanach,* or Bible. The first five books of the Bible are called the Torah, which means "teaching." Many Jewish people believe that God gave these five books directly to Moses.

The Torah includes some of humanity's greatest stories. It tells us that God created the world in six days, then rested on the seventh. It tells the stories of Adam and Eve in the Garden of Eden; of their son Cain killing his brother, Abel; of Noah and the ark. The Torah tells Jews how they should live their lives, and it tells the history of their people.

THE TEN COMMANDMENTS

Thou shalt have no other gods before me.
Thou shalt not make thyself a graven image.
Thou shalt not take the name of the Lord thy God in vain.
Remember the Sabbath day, to keep it holy.
Honor thy father and thy mother.
Thou shalt not murder.
Thou shalt not commit adultery.
Thou shalt not steal.
Thou shalt not bear false witness against thy neighbor.
Thou shalt not covet.

The Torah is the most important object in every synagogue, or Jewish meeting place of worship. It is handwritten in Hebrew, the ancient language of the Jews, on long scrolls of parchment paper. During worship services led by a rabbi—the spiritual leader of the synagogue—worshipers read out loud from the Torah.

THE NATION OF ISRAEL

In ancient times, Canaan was divided into two kingdoms, Israel and Judea. The people of Judea were called Judeans. The word Jew comes from this word. Jerusalem was the holy city, or religious center, of Judea.

At different times in history, invading armies conquered Jerusalem and drove the Jews into exile. Eventually, Jews settled all over the world. In foreign countries, they were often treated badly for practicing their religion. The worst horror took place in this century, when Nazi Germans and their supporters killed six million European Jews between 1933 and 1945. We have come to call this mass murder the Holocaust.

Throughout the centuries, though, Judaism has miraculously survived. After the Holocaust, Jews from many places returned to their ancient Promised Land, then called Palestine, and founded the nation of Israel there in 1948. Today, Jews all over the world hope that Israel will remain a safe home for their people and their religion.

▲WORSHIPERS PRAY BEFORE ONE OF JUDAISM'S HOLIEST SITES—THE WESTERN WALL IN JERUSALEM, ONCE CALLED THE WAILING WALL. THE WALL IS PART OF THE JEWISH TEMPLE DESTROYED ALMOST TWO THOUSAND YEARS AGO BY THE ROMANS.

◄ THE TORAH SCROLLS ARE KEPT AT THE FRONT OF THE SYNAGOGUE IN A DECORATED CABINET CALLED THE ARK. ON THE WALL ABOVE THE ARK IN THIS PICTURE, AT A SYNAGOGUE IN NEW YORK CITY, ARE MODELS OF THE STONE TABLETS ON WHICH THE TEN COMMANDMENTS WERE ORIGINALLY WRITTEN.

INSTEAD OF ATTENDING PUBLIC SCHOOLS, MANY ORTHODOX JEWISH CHILDREN GO TO A RELIGIOUS SCHOOL CALLED A YESHIVA. HERE THEY STUDY THE SAME SUBJECTS AS PUBLIC SCHOOL STUDENTS—HISTORY, MATH, SCIENCE—AND THEY ALSO LEARN HEBREW, ONE OF THE OLDEST LANGUAGES IN THE WORLD, ALONG WITH JEWISH RELIGIOUS TEACHINGS.

The most basic beliefs of Judaism, such as the belief in a single, all-powerful God and the laws of the Ten Commandments, have not changed for thousands of years. But since the 1800s Judaism has branched into three large groups: Orthodox, Reform, and Conservative Judaism.

Orthodox Jews practice the traditions of Judaism in the way they have been practiced for nearly two thousand years. They believe that the Torah was given directly to Moses by God. Among the rules they follow are the kosher laws, developed from the Torah about the food they eat. For example, these rules forbid Jews from eating shellfish or pork.

Orthodox Jewish men always wear a head covering called a yarmulke as a sign of respect to God. During daily worship services in Orthodox synagogues, men and women sit apart, and prayers are always said in Hebrew.

Reform Jews try to make Judaism fit into the modern world. Most Reform Jews do not follow special food laws. Men do not always wear yarmulkes, and prayer services are conducted in other languages as well as Hebrew. Most Reform synagogues hold services only on holidays and Saturdays.

Conservative Jews are "in the middle." They are more traditional than Reform Jews, but not as strict as Orthodox Jews.

For centuries, holidays and traditions have been an essential part of Jewish life. The most important Jewish holiday is the weekly Sabbath, called *Shabbat* in Hebrew. According to the Jewish creation story, God created the world in six days, then rested on the seventh. So the Sabbath, observed on the seventh day of the week, or Saturday, is also a day of rest. Many Jews do not work or travel or carry money on the Sabbath. It is a time for families to gather for worship, study, and relaxation.

There are yearly holidays that celebrate events in the history of the Jews. In autumn, on the Jewish New Year—called Rosh Hashanah in Hebrew—Jews celebrate God's creation of the world. Ten days later comes the solemn holy day of Yom Kippur, or Day of Atonement. For twenty-four hours, adult family members do not eat or drink, and they atone—pray to be forgiven—for all their wrongdoings of the past year.

A FAMILY OF ORTHODOX JEWS CELEBRATES SUKKOT IN A SPECIALLY BUILT HUT CALLED A SUKKAH.

Soon after Yom Kippur is the festival of Sukkot, a celebration of bountiful harvests. During this week-long holiday, many families eat their meals in homemade huts called *sukkahs*. Some families build the *sukkah* themselves; others go to a *sukkah* at their temple. The *sukkah* symbolizes the shelters made by the Israelites during their wandering in the desert.

Other holidays also honor events in ancient Jewish history. The eight-day holiday of Chanukah, which usually falls in December, celebrates the time when a small band of Jews drove a mighty army out of ancient Jerusalem. On each night of the holiday, families light a candle in a Chanukah menorah—a nine-branched candleholder—to commemorate the story of the miracle of a small container of oil that burned for eight days.

The spring holiday of Purim celebrates the time Queen Esther saved the Jews of ancient Persia from destruction by a powerful, wicked man named Haman. The biblical Book of Esther is read aloud in the synagogue, and children sometimes dress up and reenact the story.

On Purim, Jewish children dress in costumes to celebrate the story of Queen Esther.

Later in the spring, Jews observe the eight days of Passover, or Pesach, in honor of Moses' leading the Israelites out of Egypt. During a special Passover dinner called a Seder, families read aloud the story of the Israelites leaving Egypt from a book called the Haggadah. They eat certain foods that symbolize aspects of the ancient story: a flat bread called matzoh represents the fact that the Israelites left in a hurry and didn't have time to let their bread rise; bitter herbs represent their sad lives as slaves.

Shavuot, which comes fifty days after Passover, commemorates the giving of the Ten Commandments to Moses.

Like members of nearly all religions, Jews hold a special ceremony to celebrate the passage of a boy into manhood. The ceremony usually takes place on the first Sabbath after a boy's thirteenth birthday. At that time the boy celebrates becoming Bar Mitzvah, which means "a son of the commandments." He reads aloud from the

A YOUNG WOMAN IN NEW YORK READS FROM THE TORAH AS SHE PREPARES TO BECOME BAT MITZVAH. SHE IS HOLDING A *YAD*, A SILVER POINTER USED TO HELP PEOPLE KEEP THEIR PLACE WHILE READING FROM THE TORAH AND TO PROTECT THE SURFACE FROM FINGER MARKS.

IN ISRAEL, A YOUNG MAN CARRIES A TORAH SCROLL ON HIS WAY TO HIS BAR MITZVAH CEREMONY.

Torah. Then family and friends gather for a festive meal. Many non-Orthodox girls go through a similar ceremony when they become Bat Mitzvah, or "a daughter of the commandments."

When Jewish families celebrate holidays, festivals, and important life events, they feel close not only to each other and to God but also to Jews everywhere. They feel connected to their history and to their wise and brave ancestors—to Moses and the ancient Israelites, to a shepherd named Abraham and his wife, Sarah.

CHRISTIANITY

"I AM THE WAY, AND THE TRUTH, AND THE LIFE;

NO ONE COMES TO THE FATHER BUT BY ME."

—NEW TESTAMENT: JOHN 14:6

Almost two thousand years after Abraham lived, the land of Judea was ruled by Rome. Many Jews hoped that a divine savior, or Messiah, would come to free them and bring peace.

According to Christian scriptures, or sacred writings, an angel named Gabriel appeared to a Jewish woman named Mary. Gabriel told Mary that she had been chosen to give birth to the Messiah. The baby would be named Jesus, which means "to save."

Soon afterward, Mary and her husband, Joseph, visited the crowded town of Bethlehem and were forced to seek shelter in a humble stable. There, Mary gave birth to the baby Jesus. No one knows the exact date of Jesus' birth, but Christians celebrate it every year at Christmas, on December twenty-fifth.

◄ IN HUNGARY, A YOUNG CATHOLIC GIRL TAKES HER FIRST COMMUNION.

༄

Jesus was raised in the religion of Judaism. When he was a young man, he began talking to people about God. He spoke about God in a loving, familiar way. He called God his father and taught people to do the same in their prayers. Jesus told people that because God loved all his children equally, they should love their enemies as well as their friends.

Jesus visited the poorest people and those whom others scorned as sinners and outcasts, teaching about God's great love. He comforted the sad. He healed the sick. He made friends with those who had no friends. Many people began to love Jesus. They gathered in great crowds to hear him teach, and they followed him through the streets and sang his praises.

As the crowds grew, local Jewish leaders became concerned. They heard that Jesus was claiming to be the king of the Jews. Jesus was brought before the Roman authorities, who sentenced him to be crucified, or hung from a cross, a common way in those times to execute the worst criminals. Christians remember the terrible day of Jesus' crucifixion on the holy day of Good Friday. It is a sad, serious day for Christians. They attend long church services and grieve over Jesus' painful death.

Jesus died on the cross in Jerusalem. But according to his followers, three days after his death several women visited his tomb and discovered that his body was missing. Then an angel appeared before them and declared, "He is risen!" The angel's words meant that God had resurrected Jesus, or raised him from the dead.

Every year, on the first Sunday after the first full moon of spring, Christians celebrate Jesus' resurrection. This day is called Easter. It is the most important Christian holy day of the year because the Resurrection is the most important event in the life of Jesus. It is the victory of life over death.

A WOODEN CRUCIFIX MADE IN SPAIN IN THE ELEVENTH CENTURY. THE CRUCIFIX IS THE MOST IMPORTANT SYMBOL OF CHRISTIANITY.

Not long after Jesus' death, his followers reported that Jesus had returned from the dead and appeared before them. They had seen him by the roadside; they had seen him standing on the shores of a lake in Judea. One day he spoke to them on a mountaintop and said that the Holy Spirit, or God's spirit, would soon visit them and give them the power to spread his teachings. Then, according to his followers, Jesus was taken up into heaven and disappeared into the clouds.

Christianity teaches that about fifty days after the Resurrection many Jewish people traveled to Jerusalem from other lands for a religious festival. Jesus' followers were meeting in a room in Jerusalem to observe the holiday when suddenly they heard a mighty rushing wind. Then the Holy Spirit entered each of them, and they all began speaking in other languages—the languages of the various people visiting Jerusalem for the festival. Jesus' followers could now speak to the visitors in their native languages and tell them about Jesus.

After this event, which Christians call Pentecost, Jesus' apostles, or followers, were filled with great wisdom and knowledge and energy. They believed that Jesus was still with them, helping them spread the good news, or gospel, about him.

The apostles carried the gospel from Jerusalem out into the world, converting many Jews and non-Jews to the new religion of Christianity.

To help spread the word about Jesus, some of his first followers began writing about him. Because Christianity was so deeply connected to Judaism, these writings were added to the *Tanach*, the Bible of the Jews. Christians began to call the *Tanach* the Old Testament. They called the Christian writings the New Testament. The first four books of the New Testament—Matthew, Mark, Luke, and John—are called the Gospels and tell about the life of Jesus.

Both Judaism and Christianity teach that there is only one true God. But Christianity also teaches the doctrine of the Trinity. This is the belief that there are three aspects of the divine: God, the Father, who created the world; his Son, Jesus Christ, who is the champion and defender of the world; and the Holy Spirit, God's presence on earth, which continues to work in the world and make it a place of peace and goodwill.

As Christians spread the news about Jesus Christ, many people found hope, comfort, and inspiration in his life and teachings. Today, Christianity is the most widely practiced religion in the world, with almost two billion followers.

St. Peter's Church in Vatican City, Rome. Vatican City is the home of the Pope and the center of the Roman Catholic Church.

About a thousand years ago, the Christian religion split into two groups: Roman Catholic and Orthodox. Today, more than half of the world's Christians are Roman Catholic. Though they live all over the world, they look to the Pope in Rome as their leader.

Orthodox Christians live mainly in Russia, Greece, and many eastern European and western Asian countries, as well as the United States. Since the eleventh century they have regarded the city of Constantinople (now Istanbul, Turkey) as their official center, and their highest church leaders are called patriarchs.

About five hundred years ago, a German priest named Martin Luther tried to make changes in the Roman Catholic Church in his country. The Church resisted the changes and expelled the Lutherans (the followers of Luther). But Luther's teachings encouraged other groups to protest against what they saw as the injustices of the Church, eventually resulting in hundreds of groups that came to be called Protestant. The largest of these are the Lutheran, Presbyterian, Methodist, Baptist, and Episcopalian churches.

There can be many differences between one Christian group, or denomination, and another. Worship can be silent and serious, as in a Quaker service. It can be highly emotional, as in a Pentecostal service. It can be formal and mysterious, with incense and candles, as in an Orthodox service.

Most Christians, however, share certain practices. Worshipers meet regularly to celebrate their faith and help each other follow Jesus' teachings. They meet on Sunday, the Lord's Day, the Day of Resurrection. They meet in a church, where everyone sings and prays together.

▶An Orthodox priest holding an aspergillum (a rattle-like utensil used to sprinkle holy water) and an incense box. Incense is burned during church services; the smoke symbolizes prayers rising from earth to heaven.

A Mennonite church service in Pennsylvania. The Mennonites are a Protestant group who follow old religious and social traditions and live in close-knit rural communities.

THE LORD'S PRAYER

Our Father, who art in heaven,
hallowed be thy name.
Thy kingdom come,
thy will be done,
on earth as it is in heaven.
Give us this day our daily bread.
And forgive us our trespasses,
as we forgive those
who trespass against us.
And lead us not into temptation,
but deliver us from evil.
For thine is the kingdom, and
the power, and the glory,
forever and ever.

(Roman Catholics and some others do not include the last three lines.)

A Baptist choir, or group of singers, in Brooklyn, New York.

Most worshipers also listen to a religious leader, such as a Protestant minister or a Catholic priest, give regular sermons, or talks, based on the Bible's teachings. And almost all groups recite the Lord's Prayer, the only prayer that Jesus taught his followers.

Most Christians practice special religious rituals called sacraments. Two of these sacraments—baptism and Holy Communion—are based on events in the life of Jesus Christ.

The word *baptism* means "to wash." Even the earliest religions held the belief that washing in sacred water would purify people. According to the New Testament, Jesus was baptized in the River Jordan by a man named John the Baptist. While Jesus was being baptized, the Holy Spirit appeared in the form of a dove, and a voice from heaven said, "This is my beloved Son."

Later, Jesus instructed his followers to spread out into the world and baptize people of all nations "in the name of the Father, and of the Son, and of the Holy Spirit."

These words are still used in all Christian baptisms. The ceremony represents a rebirth to a new spiritual life.

The sacrament of Holy Communion, or Eucharist, comes from an event that occurred just before the Crucifixion. At the Last Supper—the last meal that Jesus shared with his twelve closest followers—Jesus said that he would be leaving them soon. Then he did a mysterious thing: He gave them bread to eat and said, "This is my body"; and he gave them wine to drink and said, "This is my blood."

Communion reenacts this event. During Communion, Christians eat a wafer of bread while the priest or minister repeats the words of Jesus, "This is my body." They take a sip of wine or grape juice while the minister or priest repeats, "This is my blood."

Some churches serve Communion once a month; others serve it every day. Most Christians consider Communion to be an important ritual. Communion helps them feel a oneness with Jesus Christ, with his goodness and wisdom, his courage and loving-kindness. In sharing Communion, Christians feel united with each other as well.

▶In the Roman Catholic Church, newborns are baptized by having water sprinkled on their foreheads.

ISLAM

"IN THE NAME OF ALLAH, THE BENEFICENT, THE MERCIFUL!"

—KORAN, FIRST VERSE

Just as Christianity began with the teachings of a single person, so did the religion of Islam. The founder of Islam was born almost six hundred years after Jesus. His name was Muhammad, and he lived in the city of Mecca, in the land of Arabia, which we now call Saudi Arabia.

At that time, the people of Arabia did not believe in a single God, as the Jews and Christians did. They believed in many gods and goddesses, whom they worshiped in the form of stone statues called idols. Desert tribes and merchants traveled from far and wide to Mecca, Arabia's holy city, to worship the idols and to pray to Arabia's most sacred object—the Black Stone, a mysterious stone believed to have fallen from the sky. The Black Stone was located in the holiest area of Mecca, in a shrine known as the Kaaba.

◄ A BOY IN AFGHANISTAN READING THE KORAN, THE HOLY BOOK OF ISLAM.

Though he was a successful merchant, Muhammad was not happy with life in Mecca. He thought that people cared too much about money. He was disturbed by all the fighting, gambling, and drinking in the city, and he questioned the worship of idols. He wondered what the true religion was.

Muhammad spent many long, lonely hours in a desert cave, praying for answers. One day when he was about forty, he heard a voice tell him to "recite"—to listen to the words of God and repeat them.

Fearing for his sanity, Muhammad rushed home and told his wife, Kadijah, what had happened. Eventually, Kadijah and other members of his family helped him understand that he was going to be a prophet—a person who receives revelations, or messages from God, then tells people what God has said.

For the next twenty years, Muhammad heard the mysterious voice again and again. He believed that it was the angel Gabriel, giving him messages from Allah. Allah was the chief god of the many gods and goddesses whom the Arabs worshiped. But the voice said that Allah was all-powerful and was the one and only God.

THE BADSHAHI MOSQUE IN PAKISTAN IS ONE OF THE LARGEST MOSQUES IN THE WORLD. IT HOLDS NEARLY 100,000 WORSHIPERS.

THE DOME OF THE ROCK

Islam has close connections to Judaism and Christianity. Muslims trace their ancestry back to Abraham, and they respect Hebrew and Christian scriptures.

Jerusalem is a holy city for Muslims as well as Christians and Jews. The Dome of the Rock, which stands near the Western Wall in Jerusalem, was built on the spot where, according to followers of Islam, the angel Gabriel brought Muhammad up to heaven to meet with Abraham, Moses, and Jesus. This golden-domed building, erected in 691, is sacred to Muslims and is considered by many to be the most beautiful structure in all of Jerusalem.

Muhammad tried to share Allah's messages with the people of Mecca. He told them that Allah was all-seeing and all-knowing, and that everyone was equal in Allah's eyes. Muhammad also told people how to live their lives. He told them not to drink or gamble and to be kind to widows, orphans, and animals.

Many people in Mecca did not like Muhammad's message. For one thing, merchants made a great deal of money selling religious articles to idol worshipers. Muhammad was pelted with stones and dirt and threatened with death many times, until finally, in the year 622, he fled to Medina, a city north of Mecca.

In Medina, many people were eager to hear Muhammad's teachings. There he built the first mosque—the Islamic house of worship—and formed the first Islamic community.

Eventually, Muhammad and his army of followers returned to Mecca and took over the city. They destroyed all the idols and turned the area around the Kaaba into a mosque. Then Muhammad dedicated the mosque to Allah.

Those who accepted Muhammad as God's prophet came to be called Muslims. Their religion came to be called Islam, which means "to surrender to God," or to submit oneself completely to God's will.

By the time Muhammad died, all of Arabia had surrendered to Allah, the all-powerful God of the universe.

A MUEZZIN, OR CALLER, CALLS MUSLIMS TO PRAYER FROM A TOWER ATTACHED TO A MOSQUE, CALLED A MINARET.

To show respect for Allah, Muslims wash their hands, feet, arms, and faces in a special part of the mosque before praying. Pictures of living beings are forbidden by the Koran, for fear that Muslims might worship these images rather than Allah, so mosques around the world have been decorated with beautiful designs called arabesques. This one is in the city of Fez in Morocco.

Muhammad taught in beautiful, poetic language that he said came directly from Allah. He himself could not read or write, but his followers wrote down his revelations on stones, leaves, and the bones of animals. Later, these writings were gathered into a holy book called the Koran, the Arabic word for "recitation." The Koran also includes many stories that appear in Jewish and Christian scriptures.

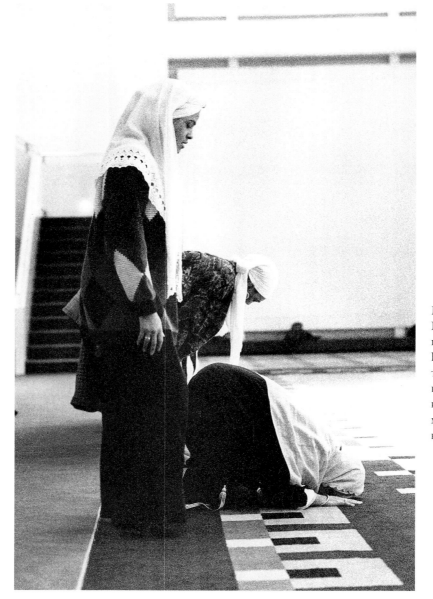

MUSLIM WOMEN AT THE ISLAMIC CULTURAL CENTER IN NEW YORK CITY. FEMALE WORSHIPERS COVER THEIR HEADS AS A SIGN OF RESPECT FOR ALLAH, AND PRAY IN A SECTION OF THE MOSQUE THAT IS SEPARATE FROM THE MEN.

Children in northern Africa studying verses from the Koran. Islam has been a presence in Africa for a thousand years.

A YOUNG MUSLIM
BOY KNEELING IN
A CHICAGO MOSQUE
DURING EID-UL-FITR,
THE CELEBRATION
AT THE END OF
RAMADAN. THERE
ARE OVER THREE
MILLION MUSLIMS IN
NORTH AMERICA.

Today Muslims everywhere consider the Koran the divine word of God. It may also be the most memorized book in the world, as many Muslim children first learn to read by reciting daily from the Koran.

Although Islam is the youngest of the seven major religions, it is the second largest religion in the world. Nearly one billion people today are Muslims.

Muslims believe in five duties, which are called the five pillars of Islam. Just as the pillars of a building help support its roof, the five pillars help support the Islamic religion.

The first duty is *shahada*, or declaration of faith. Every Muslim must say these words and deeply believe them: "There is no God but Allah, and Muhammad is his Prophet and Messenger."

The second duty is *salat*, or prayer. Every Muslim must pray at least five times a day: at dawn, noon, midafternoon, sunset, and before bed. Wherever they happen to be at these times, worshipers face the Kaaba at Mecca, Islam's holiest city, and pray.

At each prayer time, a muezzin, or caller, climbs up a tower in the local mosque and calls out a chant to remind Muslims to pray. Nearly every Islamic neighborhood has a mosque, which means "a place of kneeling." Worshipers may pray inside the mosque at any time. On Fridays, Muslims join together at the mosque in a special session of community worship. In those sessions, the imam, or mosque leader, recites from the Koran and gives a sermon.

The third pillar of Islam is *zakat*, or almsgiving. Every Muslim should give a part of his or her income to the poor.

The fourth pillar is *sawm*, or fasting. Muslims fast during the holy month of Ramadan, which celebrates the month that the Koran was revealed to Muhammad. During Ramadan, adult Muslims do not eat or drink during the daylight hours. Activity slows down for the day, and people take more time to pray and concentrate on their love and need for Allah. Fasting during Ramadan not only teaches self-discipline, it also makes Muslims feel greater sympathy for the poor.

During Ramadan, Muslims celebrate the Night of Power—the night Muhammad first heard the voice of the angel Gabriel. The joyful Feast of Fast Breaking, or Eid-ul-Fitr, celebrates the end of Ramadan. For three days, families and friends gather to share food and gifts. In many Islamic countries, the Eid is a national holiday.

The fifth pillar is *hajj*, or pilgrimage. A pilgrimage is a special journey to a sacred place. All Muslims are expected to make a pilgrimage to the holy city of Mecca once during their lives. Dressed in white, the pilgrims perform certain rituals while they are there. They go to the Great Mosque and walk around the Kaaba seven times, each time kissing the sacred Black Stone in its wall. And they celebrate the Feast of Sacrifice, which involves the killing of sheep, goats, or camels as an offering made to Allah. The meat from the sacrificed animals is often given to the poor.

Only Muslims are allowed to enter Mecca. Every year, about two million come to the holy city from all over the world—from Africa, Indonesia, Bangladesh, Pakistan, the United States, and many other lands. In Mecca, different nationalities come together like members of the same family. The pilgrimage unites Muslims in their great love for Allah and in their respect for Allah's human messenger, the prophet Muhammad.

▶ PILGRIMS PRAY AT THE KAABA, THE SQUARE BUILDING IN THE CENTER OF THE PICTURE, WHERE THE SACRED BLACK STONE IS LOCATED. MUSLIMS REGARD THE KAABA, IN MECCA, SAUDI ARABIA, AS THE HOLIEST SPOT ON EARTH.

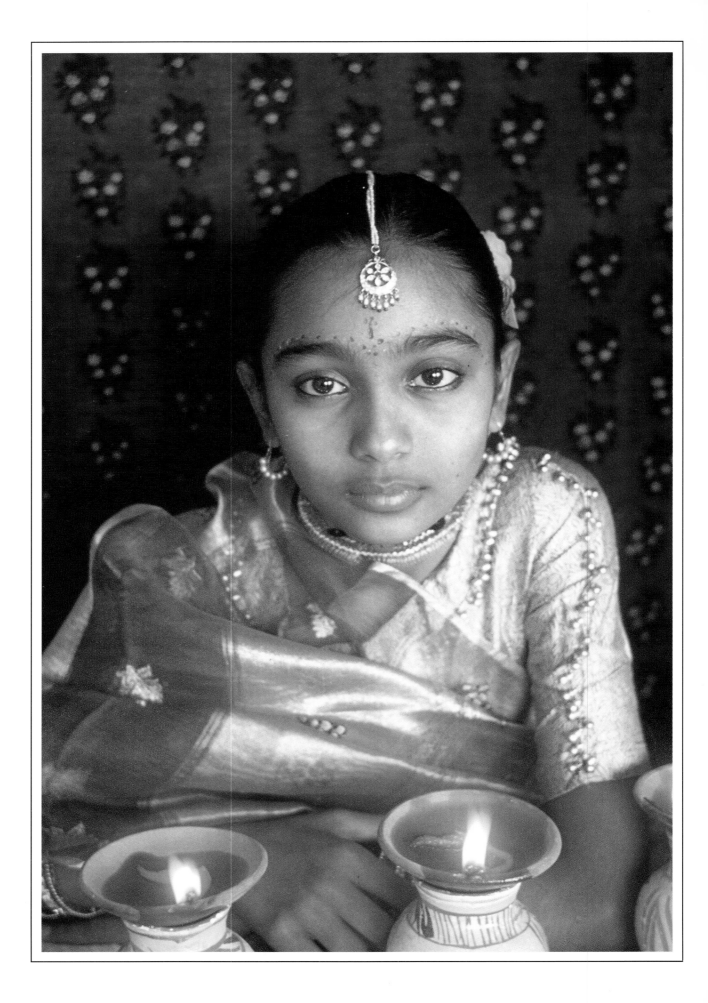

HINDUISM

"O GODS! ALL YOUR NAMES AND FORMS ARE TO BE REVERED,
SALUTED, AND ADORED."

—RIG VEDA X. 63. 2

In the countries of India and Nepal, the sights and sounds of Hinduism are every-where—from colorful roadside shrines to the constant tinkling of temple bells. Hinduism is not only the major religion in these countries, it is also a way of life that determines what kind of jobs people have, what friends they associate with, what foods they eat, and whom they marry.

Unlike Christianity and Islam, Hinduism was not founded by one person. Rather, it developed over many centuries, embracing the traditions of different races and cultures. Today Hinduism has more than 750 million followers, making it the third largest religion in the world, after Christianity and Islam.

◄ A YOUNG HINDU GIRL WITH LAMPS LIT FOR THE DIWALI FESTIVAL.

Hindus believe in a universal spirit called Brahman, which means the "World-Soul." According to Hindu writings, the World-Soul is all things—man, woman, child, "the dark-blue bee, the green parrot with red eyes, thunderclouds and seas," and everything else in the universe.

Hinduism has more than 300 million different deities, or gods and goddesses. But for most Hindus, all the gods and goddesses are simply the countless different faces of Brahman, the World-Soul.

Some of the important early Hindu gods were the fire god, who rode a ram; the thunder god with a thousand eyes; and the goddess of dawn, who drove seven cows. Today, the most important gods and goddesses of Hinduism are Vishnu, Shakti, and Shiva.

Vishnu is a kind and loving god who sometimes comes to earth in the form of a human known as Krishna or Rama.

The goddess Shakti has many forms—among them, Sarasvati, the goddess of wisdom and learning; Lakshmi, the goddess of wealth and good fortune; and Durga, the goddess who protects the universe.

The god Shiva destroys old life to make room for the new. Shiva lurks on battlefields and is often shown wearing a necklace of skulls.

One of the most popular gods is Ganesh, the elephant-headed god. According to Hindu legend, Ganesh was once a boy who had been formed out of flour and oil. One day his mother told him to guard her door and not let anyone in. When Ganesh blocked the way of the god Shiva, Shiva smashed the boy's head into a thousand pieces. Ganesh's mother demanded that her son's head be restored, but the first head found was that of an elephant. To soothe the mother's sorrow, Shiva granted the elephant-headed boy the power to remove obstacles. When Hindus begin a new venture, they often pray to Ganesh, asking for his help.

神心上油

THE ELEPHANT-HEADED GOD GANESH. WORSHIPERS PRAY TO GANESH WHEN THEY NEED HELP WITH A NEW
UNDERTAKING, SUCH AS STARTING A JOB OR MOVING TO A NEW PLACE.

Hindus believe that special places in nature can also be gods or goddesses. The Ganges River, which flows more than 1,500 miles through the heart of India, is thought to be a goddess who came to earth from the hair of Shiva. Just as Muslims make pilgrimages to Mecca, Hindus make pilgrimages to the Ganges. They line the banks of the river by the hundreds, believing that her water will wash away their sins and help cure their illnesses. They hope that after they die, their relatives will throw their ashes into the Ganges.

Certain animals are sacred to the Hindus, too. The most sacred is the cow. Hindus honor her because she gives important gifts. Not only does she pull plows and carts and give milk and cheese, but her dung is an essential source of fuel. It is strictly against Hindu teachings to kill a cow, and some Hindus would rather starve than eat the meat of a cow. As a sign of respect for *all* animals, many Hindus do not eat meat of any kind. They also don't believe in hunting or offering animals as sacrifices.

Monkeys are also sacred creatures. According to Hindu tradition, the god

BATHERS AT THE
GANGES RIVER.

Vishnu visited earth as Rama and married a woman named Sita. When Sita was stolen by a demon king, a monkey named Hanuman helped rescue her. Hindu temples dedicated to Hanuman treat monkeys as special guests.

AT A TEMPLE DEDICATED TO HANUMAN IN BENARES, INDIA, MONKEYS ARE TREATED AS SPECIAL GUESTS.

Hinduism teaches that all creatures—human and animal—have a soul, or an invisible part that lives on after death. After a person dies, the soul is released from the body as if the body were a worn-out robe. Hindus believe that fire helps to release the soul, so the body is cremated, or burned, as quickly as possible after death. Relatives often throw the ashes into a holy river, such as the Ganges.

WORSHIPERS AT A HINDU TEMPLE.

After the body is cremated, Hindus believe that the soul is reincarnated, or born again into a new body. If you are very good in this life, you might be born again as a person with remarkable talents. If you are bad, you might come back as a worm or an ant. This idea is called karma. The law of karma teaches that "from good must come good; and from evil, evil." In other words, your actions now will determine what happens to you in the future, both in this life and the next.

Hinduism teaches that a soul goes through reincarnation again and again—until finally it is freed from life on earth and joins the World-Soul, which endures forever and is without beginning and without end.

෴

Long ago, a Hindu legend explained how society should be ordered. The legend said that out of the mouth of a great god came the holiest people, the priests and scholars. From the god's arms came the rulers and warriors. From the god's thighs came the merchants and farmers. And from the god's feet came the servants and laborers. These four groups are called castes, and most Hindus are born into one caste or another. There are people, however, who do not belong to any caste. They are called "untouchables," and they perform some of the less desirable jobs in society, such as sweeping the streets and cleaning bathrooms.

According to Hindu tradition, people must marry and work within their own caste. If your father raised goats, he would teach you to raise goats, too. You would not be able to become a lawyer, for example, or a teacher, or even marry one. Some believe that the caste system is unfair because it means that people are not treated equally. But many Hindus defend it, saying that for centuries it has helped their society run smoothly.

The followers of Hinduism worship individually, not in congregations as Jews, Christians, and Muslims do. Most Hindu homes have a shrine—a special place for worshiping the gods. Part of the family's daily routine is to pray at the shrine before a statue or a picture of their chosen deity. Several times a day, family members place gifts of food or flowers before the statue. They might also light a candle or burn incense. This simple ceremony is called puja, which means "honor" or "worship."

Hindus also worship in temples. There is a temple in each Indian town, usually devoted to one main god, such as Vishnu or Shiva. Worshipers ring a bell at the temple entrance as they walk in. Then they place flowers or sweets before the images of the gods and offer silent prayers. In the countryside, villagers worship at simple outdoor shrines, where they pray to a local goddess or "guardian of the village."

Another form of daily worship is the practice of meditation. In meditation, a person sits in a special position and concentrates on breathing. By repeating a simple word or phrase, such as the sacred syllable *om*, one grows calm, peaceful, and alert. The goal of meditation is to help a person feel united with the source of all life.

YOGA EXERCISE INVOLVES SOME EXTRAORDINARY POSITIONS, OR POSTURES. MANY PEOPLE WHO PRACTICE YOGA DO NOT CONSIDER THEMSELVES HINDUS. THEY SIMPLY ENJOY IT AS A RELAXING FORM OF EXERCISE.

Hindus also practice a kind of exercise called yoga. Yoga involves physical positions and breathing exercises to discipline both the body and the mind. Yoga is good for a person's health, but mainly it teaches the self-control needed for a full spiritual life.

Just as the Bar and Bat Mitzvah ceremonies honor Jewish boys and girls as they become young adults, there is a ritual, called the sacred thread ceremony, that honors Hindu boys at this important time in their lives. For Hindu boys—as for Jewish children—the ceremony also marks their entrance into religious life.

THE SACRED THREAD CEREMONY. ONLY BOYS OF THE TOP THREE CASTES ARE ALLOWED TO COMPLETE THE CEREMONY. THERE IS NO SIMILAR RITUAL FOR YOUNG GIRLS, BUT WOMEN PLAY A VITAL ROLE IN HINDUISM.

The sacred thread ceremony is held only for boys from the upper three castes and sometimes takes place on the day before the boy's wedding. A guru, or holy teacher, hangs a sacred thread over the boy's left shoulder and under his right arm. From then on, the boy will wear the thread and be called "twice born," because he has been born once into the world and a second time into the religious life.

Throughout the year, there are many Hindu festivals. Among the most joyous are Holi and Diwali. Holi, which falls in March or April, celebrates the end of winter. People dance in the streets and throw colored water at each other. Diwali, which comes in October or November, closes the Hindu year and begins the new year. Diwali is also called the Festival of Lights. As night falls, Hindus light many small lamps to frighten away demons and to welcome the return of the god Rama, who had been forced to flee his kingdom.

There are countless groups within Hinduism. But they are all bound together by a huge collection of sacred Hindu writings. The oldest writings are called the Vedas, which means "books of knowledge." The Vedas were written more than three thousand years ago and are filled with wisdom about the universe. One of the most striking teachings of the Vedas is that all religions are true—they all lead to the same goal, though by different paths.

▶ Young Hindu girls at a Diwali festival in New York City. There are more than a million Hindus living in the United States and Canada.

BUDDHISM

"BE YE LAMPS UNTO YOURSELVES."

—BUDDHA'S FAREWELL ADDRESS, FROM THE MAHAPARINIBBANA SUTTANA

Five hundred years before Jesus was born, a young prince named Siddhartha Gautama was born in the country we now call Nepal. Siddhartha was raised as a Hindu. He read the great writings of Hinduism and practiced Hindu rituals.

Siddhartha had little knowledge of the world outside his luxurious palace. One day when he went out among his people, he was greatly disturbed by four sights: a very old man, a very sick man, a man who had just died, and a wandering monk, or holy man.

The first three sights sorrowed the young prince. He wondered, why do people grow old? Why do they get sick? Why do they suffer and die? Siddhartha decided that he should become a monk himself, so that he could go into the world and search for answers to his questions.

Siddhartha took off his royal garments and put on a faded orange robe. He shaved his hair and his beard. Then he left his palace forever and set out in search of wisdom.

◄ A YOUNG BUDDHIST BOY IN MYANMAR (BURMA). HE WILL LIVE AS A BUDDHIST MONK FOR SEVERAL YEARS; THEN HE WILL RETURN TO HIS VILLAGE.

Siddhartha wandered for six years. Then one night when the moon was full, he stopped to rest under a fig tree. He vowed not to move until he had found answers to his questions.

Siddhartha sat in a cross-legged position. He closed his eyes and began practicing a form of yoga meditation. He concentrated on the great Hindu teachings. He thought about the endless cycle of death and rebirth. He thought about human pain and suffering.

During his meditation, Siddhartha had a revelation—a sudden divine understanding—that explained everything to him. He understood that people could find an end to suffering. To followers of Buddhism, this new and powerful insight is

STATUE OF
BUDDHA IN JAPAN

known as the Enlightenment. When it happened to Siddhartha, he became known as the Buddha.

The Buddha believed that other people could achieve enlightenment as well—but before they did, they had to free themselves from all their worldly desires, such as the desire for riches, for a good job, for a wife or a husband. This special freedom is known as detachment. The Buddha's understanding of suffering and detachment is called dharma. The dharma represents all the teachings of Buddhism.

The basic message of the Buddha's teaching is summed up in the Four Noble Truths. They are clear and simple: All lives are filled with suffering. Suffering comes from a desire for worldly things. Suffering ends when desire ends. People can learn to end desire by following eight rules.

The eight rules, known as the Noble Eightfold Path, are:

Right understanding: Be aware of the Buddha's teachings.

Right intentions: Try to follow these teachings wholeheartedly.

Right speech: Say nothing to harm others.

Right action: Do nothing to harm any living creature.

Right livelihood: Choose a job that hurts no living thing.

Right effort: Strive to become a good person.

Right mindfulness: Learn to control all your thoughts and
    emotions in order to quiet your mind.

Right concentration: Practice the deepest meditation, which leads
    to the highest state of enlightenment, known as Nirvana.

Nirvana is something that happens when one is completely released from suffering. It is so different from everyday life that Buddhists believe it cannot be described.

ᏮᎷᏮ

For forty-five years, the Buddha walked all over the land, teaching people how to find enlightenment. As he taught, a new religion grew around him. This religion was different from Hinduism in several ways. The Buddha taught that following the Noble Eightfold Path could be done without the long fasts and difficult yoga practices of Hindu holy men and women. This less difficult path became known as the Middle Way. Another difference was that the Buddha did not believe in the Hindu caste system. And he did not believe in worshiping the many Hindu gods and goddesses. According to one legend, someone once asked him if he were God.

"No," he said.

"Are you a saint?"

"No."

"What are you then?"

"I am awake," he said.

This is one meaning of the name Buddha: the Awakened One, one who has finally woken up to the truth.

At the age of eighty, the Buddha died from food poisoning. After his death, his fol- lowers saved some of his bones and teeth as relics—sacred religious objects— believing that his power still resided in them.

Special structures called stupas were built to house the relics. Today, there are thousands of stupas throughout Asia. Because there are a limited number of relics, most stupas house sacred writings and images instead.

Since the Buddha's death, countless images of him have been erected inside tem- ples and at outdoor shrines. These statues and images give worshipers a sense of the Buddha's loving presence.

A COSTUMED
ELEPHANT CARRIES
A TOOTH SAID TO
HAVE BELONGED TO
THE BUDDHA IN
THE ESALA
PERAHERA
FESTIVAL, HELD
EACH YEAR IN
SRI LANKA.

ᕘᘎᕘ

The Buddha organized his followers into a holy community of monks and
nuns—men and women who devoted their entire lives to their religion. For centuries after his death, monks and nuns kept Buddhism alive. They inscribed the
Buddha's wisdom on palm leaves and stored the leaves in baskets. Eventually, these
writings became part of a huge collection of Buddhist scriptures. Buddhist monks
and nuns spread the word about the Buddha's teachings, and today there are more
than 300 million Buddhists in the world, making Buddhism the world's fourth
largest religion.

Young Buddhist monks on the grounds of the Imperial Palace in Bangkok, Thailand.

▶ Statues of the Buddha in Myanmar (Burma). The statues are slightly larger than life-size.
The long ears of the images indicate the Buddha's great wisdom.

As Buddhism spread from its origins in India, it split into two different groups: Theravada Buddhism, which is practiced mainly in Southeast Asia; and Mahayana Buddhism, which is practiced mainly in Central and East Asia. Mahayana Buddhism has also spread to Europe and North America.

Theravada Buddhism teaches that monks, called arhats, are the perfect models of Buddhism. Their poverty and simplicity free them to spend their time meditating, seeking personal enlightenment. The monks wear saffron robes, much like the one that the Buddha wore. They shave their heads, as the Buddha did. They never marry. They sleep in simple dwellings called monasteries. They do not worry about making money, but depend on others to feed them. Every day, they carry their "begging bowls" from house to house, and people give them food. In return, the monks give spiritual guidance to the community.

In Theravadin countries, young men often worship by becoming monks temporarily. During the rainy season, when there is little farm work, they shave their heads, put on the faded orange robes, and carry begging bowls. Boys as young as four or five sometimes don the robes of a monk and spend a night in a monastery.

Theravada Buddhism teaches that a person must travel the path to Nirvana alone, as Prince Siddhartha did. Mahayana Buddhists, on the other hand, emphasize that people should help one another achieve Nirvana. They teach that since we have all been reincarnated, or reborn, countless times, we are all related to one another. The beggar in the street might have been your mother in a past life. The criminal might have been your brother. So before you enter Nirvana, you should help the beggar, the criminal, and all others who are suffering.

In Mahayana Buddhism, men and women who have achieved enlightenment are called Bodhisattvas. They delay entering Nirvana until they can help others do the same.

Within Mahayana Buddhism are a number of different groups, such as Vajrayana Buddhism, Zen Buddhism, and Pure Land Buddhism.

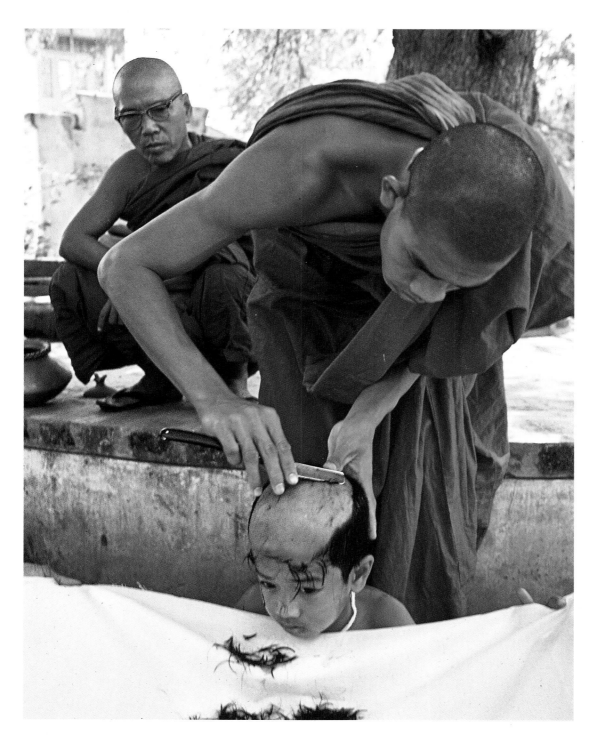

In imitation of the young Siddhartha, a Burmese boy has his head shaved. Then he will stay at a monastery for a short time.

Vajrayana Buddhism is practiced in Central Asia. Its followers believe that the more a prayer is repeated, the more powerful it becomes. A prayer can be written out thousands of times and spun on a special object called a prayer wheel. The prayer wheel repeats the prayer as it turns in the wind.

A TIBETAN BUDDHIST MAN WITH A PRAYER WHEEL.

A JAPANESE WOMAN PREPARES FOR A TEA CEREMONY. ZEN TEACHES THAT THE MOST ORDINARY ACTIVITIES, SUCH AS SERVING TEA OR KEEPING A GARDEN, ARE FILLED WITH WONDER AND MYSTERY.

A popular form of modern Buddhism is Zen, which began in China and spread to Korea and Japan. Zen Buddhism centers on meditation. Meditators are expected to sit with their eyes closed and count each breath, without thinking about other things. This sounds simple, but the mind is so restless that students often work for a long time before they can successfully meditate.

Zen can seem like a puzzling religion. Zen monks sometimes ask their students odd questions, such as "What is the sound of one hand clapping?" A riddle like this is called a koan. It is supposed to help students think and see things in a new way.

The most common form of Buddhism in Japan is Pure Land Buddhism. Followers primarily worship the Amida Buddha, the Buddha of Boundless Light. They believe that faith in Amida will lead to their rebirth in a paradise known as the Pure Land.

Many Japanese Buddhists also practice the ancient religion of Shinto. Shinto teaches that divine forces live in all things that inspire awe and wonder, such as a waterfall, a whirlpool, a mysterious cave, a beautiful stone, an exquisite insect, the wind and rain, thunder and lightning, and even a fascinating person.

Japanese Buddhists sometimes worship at Shinto shrines as well as at Buddhist temples. And religious festivals throughout the Japanese year involve a combination of Shinto, Buddhist, and Confucian practices.

One important Buddhist festival takes place each year on the first full moon of May. It is the celebration of the Buddha's birthday. In southern Asian countries, the day is marked by candlelit processions. In Japan, children carry lotus flowers and pour tea over the head of an image of the infant Buddha.

The lotus flower is an important symbol for Buddhists. In nature, the lotus grows in shallow waters, its flower emerging from the mud. In the same way, Buddhism teaches that purity can rise out of the world's suffering to blossom in the sun.

Followers of Buddhism meditate before sacred images of the Buddha kept in temples. The times of the services may vary. In some countries, services are held four times a month, at the four main phases of the moon. In other countries, public worship takes place every Sunday.

Normally, Buddhists may worship in a temple at any time. They first remove their shoes, then enter the temple and bow before an image of the Buddha. They offer gifts of flowers, food, or candles. Then they sit on the floor and pray or meditate in the peaceful atmosphere.

Buddhists also meditate before a simple shrine in their home. At home, as in the temple, sweet-smelling incense and candles are burned before a statue of the Buddha. The candlelight represents the Buddha's wisdom giving light to the world.

As a Buddhist bows each morning before the flickering flame, he or she might recite a common Buddhist prayer: "May all beings be free from sorrow."

WORSHIPERS INSIDE A BUDDHIST TEMPLE IN MYANMAR (BURMA).

CONFUCIANISM
AND TAOISM

"I AM A TRANSMITTER AND NOT A CREATOR. I BELIEVE
IN AND HAVE A PASSION FOR THE ANCIENTS."

—THE ANALECTS OF CONFUCIUS: VII. I

China is the home of the oldest civilization in the world. Today, the Communist government of China discourages its people from practicing religion. But throughout much of China's history, three religions played an important part in everyday life. They were Buddhism, Confucianism, and Taoism.

Confucianism is based on the ideas of a humble Chinese scholar named Confucius. When the Buddha was teaching in India 2,500 years ago, Confucius was teaching in China. The son of a military officer, Confucius studied music, poetry, and the writing of China's ancient sages, or wise men.

◄ KOREAN BOYS CELEBRATING CONFUCIUS'S BIRTHDAY.

For centuries, the sages had taught the Chinese people how to live a good life. But in Confucius's time, leaders had forgotten the teachings of the past. Society had fallen into chaos, and greed and violence had taken over.

Afraid that China's great civilization might be destroyed forever, Confucius began traveling around his country, teaching the wisdom of the sages.

Confucius taught the old traditions, which were based on goodness and truth. He said that government leaders should stop being so selfish and should start caring for their people the way a loving father cares for his family. He said that people should start respecting their leaders, their parents, and their ancestors; and that rich and poor children alike should get a good education.

Confucius also taught the ancient Chinese belief that everything in the universe is a combination of two forces called yin and yang. Yin is all that is cold, dark, moonlike, and mysterious. Yang is the opposite of yin—everything that is bright, warm, sunlike, and clear. All growth and change come from a combination of these two forces.

Confucius also said that all people should be courteous and kind to one another. One of his best-known sayings is: "Never do to others what you would not like them to do to you." Most major religions teach a version of this saying, which is sometimes called the golden rule.

Confucius thought of his teachings as a guide to wisdom and good behavior rather than as a religion. But after his death, temples were built to honor him, and Confucianism became the official religion of China. Applicants for government jobs had to study the books of Confucianism, and rulers relied on Confucian scholars for help and advice.

Confucius believed his duty was only to remind people of the teachings of the

▶CONFUCIUS, PAINTED BY THE SEVENTEENTH-CENTURY JAPANESE PAINTER KANO TAN'YU.

ancient sages. But he brought new meaning to the wisdom of the past. For more than two thousand years, many Chinese have considered him the wisest sage of all. A plaque in a Confucian temple in Taiwan, the main island of the Republic of China, calls Confucius "the great teacher of 10,000 generations."

Taoism began with a man named Lao-tzu, who lived during the time of Confucius. Not much is known about Lao-tzu, whose name means "Old Master." Legend says that when he was a very old man, he grew tired of war and violence and decided to leave China. He drove an ox cart to the border of the country. But a guard there recognized the wise thinker and wouldn't let him pass until he wrote down all his wisdom.

The Old Master quickly wrote his teaching in a short book that later came to be called the *Tao Te Ching*. For many centuries, the *Tao Te Ching* was one of the most important books in China.

The teaching of the *Tao Te Ching* concerns a mysterious force in the universe called the Tao. The word *Tao* means "the way," or "the road." The Tao is the infinite source of all life, and it is impossible to truly name. The more you try to name it, the more it escapes you. The Tao is often described as a flowing stream. Just as you cannot hold flowing water in your hands, you cannot grasp the Tao.

Taoism teaches that in order to live in harmony with the Tao, you should try to live a quiet and simple life close to nature. You should be humble and compassionate. You should do your work without seeking fame or fortune.

Like Confucius, Lao-tzu wasn't interested in creating a religion. But over time, his teachings were combined with Chinese folk religions—the ancient customs and religious practices of ordinary people. Taoism began to include beliefs in gods and goddesses, dragons and magicians, spells and charms. The ancient Chinese religion of ancestor veneration, or respect, also became increasingly important in Taoism.

AN IMAGE OF LAO-TZU, THE LEGENDARY FOUNDER OF TAOISM, RIDING HIS OX.

Folk tradition teaches that the ancestors connect the world of the living to the world of the gods. If people honor their ancestors, the spirits of the ancestors will protect them. During the Chinese New Year celebration, the most important Chinese religious holiday of the year, families gather to feast and honor their ancestors.

After the Chinese Communists took over China in 1949, they discouraged the

A Chinese New Year celebration in New York City. Men parade through the streets in a dragon costume, symbolizing the return of the life-giving yang force.

people of mainland China from following their traditional religions. But in Taiwan, Hong Kong, and other parts of the world, including the United States, many Chinese people still practice a combination of Confucianism, Taoism, folk religion, and Buddhism.

Each religion offers something different. Families might revere the wise Confucius and study his teachings. At the same time, they might keep a shrine to worship a Taoist god, a shrine to honor the Buddha, and a special place to honor their ancestors. For Chinese people, all these ways of worship unite to form one spiritual world.

A CHINESE WOMAN WORSHIPS AT A TEMPLE IN TAIWAN.

GLOSSARY

(Words in *italics* are defined in the glossary.)

Allah All-powerful god of Islam.

baptism Christian *sacrament* representing rebirth to a new spiritual life.

Bar Mitzvah Jewish ceremony celebrating the passage of a boy into adulthood.

Bat Mitzvah Jewish ceremony celebrating the passage of a girl into adulthood.

Bible The sacred book of Christianity, which includes the *Old Testament* and the *New Testament.*

Brahman Universal spirit, or "World-Soul," of Hinduism.

Buddha An enlightened or awakened one.

Canaan The land that God promised to Abraham.

castes Divisions of Hindu society.

Chanukah Eight-day Jewish holiday commemorating the time a small band of Jews drove a mighty army out of ancient *Jerusalem.*

Christmas Christian holiday celebrating the birth of *Jesus Christ.*

Confucius Chinese teacher who revived the wisdom of ancient sages.

dharma Truths of reality, taught by the *Buddha.*

Diwali Hindu Festival of Lights, celebrating the beginning of the new year.

Easter Christian holiday celebrating the resurrection of *Jesus Christ.*

Eid-ul-Fitr Islamic Feast of Fast Breaking, celebrating the end of *Ramadan.*

Enlightenment Buddhist term for divine understanding.

Eucharist see *Holy Communion.*

Gospels The first four books of the *New Testament,* which tell of the life of *Jesus Christ.*

guru Hindu holy teacher.

hajj Fifth pillar of Islam: holy *pilgrimage* to Mecca.

Holi Hindu holiday celebrating the end of winter.

Holy Communion Christian *sacrament* symbolizing union with *Jesus Christ.*

Israelites Descendants of Abraham, led by Moses out of Egypt.

Jerusalem Holy city for Jews, Christians, and Muslims.

Jesus Christ Holy savior of the Christian religion.

Judeans People of Judea, one of two kingdoms of *Canaan.* The word "Jew" comes from this word.

Kaaba Shrine in the holy area of *Mecca.*

karma Hindu belief that one's actions determine what happens to one in the future, both in this life and the next.

Koran The holy book of Islam, considered by Muslims to be the divine word of God.

Lao-tzu Chinese "Old Master" who wrote the *Tao Te Ching,* the most important book of Taoism.

Mahayana Form of Buddhism practiced mainly in Central and East Asia.

Mecca Holiest city of Islam, in Saudi Arabia.

Messiah The expected divine savior of the Jews, later applied by Christians to *Jesus Christ.*

muezzin Caller who summons Muslims to prayer.

Muhammad *Allah's* prophet on earth, founder of Islam.

GLOSSARY

New Testament   Christian writings, which, together with the Jewish *Tanach,* or *Old Testament,* make up the Christian *Bible*.

Nirvana   State of mind described by Buddhism as free from all suffering.

Old Testament   Christian name for the Jewish *Tanach*.

Passover   Jewish holiday commemorating Moses' leading the *Israelites* out of Egypt.

patriarchs   Highest church leaders of Orthodox Christianity.

pilgrimage   A journey to a sacred place.

Pope   Leader of the *Roman Catholic* Church.

Protestant   One of the three major divisions of Christianity (with the Orthodox and *Roman Catholic* churches).

puja   Simple Hindu ceremony of worship.

Purim   Jewish holiday celebrating Queen Esther's saving the Jews of ancient Persia.

Ramadan   Muslim holy month of fasting.

reincarnation   Hindu belief that after death the soul is born again into a new body.

Roman Catholic   Christian church headed by the *Pope* in Rome.

Rosh Hashanah   Hebrew name for the Jewish New Year, celebrating God's creation of the world.

Sabbath   Jewish weekly holiday, observed on Saturday, the seventh day of the week.

sacrament   A sacred Christian religious ritual, including *Holy Communion* and *baptism*.

salat   Second pillar of Islam: prayer.

sawm   Fourth pillar of Islam: fasting.

shahada   First pillar of Islam: a declaration of faith.

Shavuot   Jewish holiday commemorating the giving of the *Ten Commandments* to Moses.

Shinto   Ancient religion of Japan.

Siddhartha Gautama   Founder of Buddhism, who lived 2,500 years ago.

stupas   Structures built by Buddhists to house relics.

Sukkot   Jewish holiday celebrating bountiful harvests.

synagogue   Jewish meeting place for worship and study.

Tanach   Judaism's holy book made up of the *Torah*, the Prophets, and the Writings; known as the *Old Testament* in Christianity.

Tao   In Taoism, the path or "the way"; the infinite source of all life.

Tao Te Ching   Most important book of Chinese Taoism, written by *Lao-tzu*.

Ten Commandments   Ten laws that God gave to Moses to give to the *Israelites*.

Theravada   Form of Buddhism practiced mainly in Southeast Asia.

Torah   First five books of the Jewish scriptures, also called the Law; the holiest part of the Jewish *Tanach*.

Vedas   Holy writings of Hinduism, written over 3,000 years ago.

yoga   Special Hindu discipline, involving breathing and physical exercise.

Yom Kippur   Jewish holiday, the Day of Atonement.

zakat   Third pillar of Islam: giving money to the poor.

Zen   Form of Japanese Buddhism that emphasizes meditation.

JUDAISM

CHRISTIANITY
Eastern Orthodox

Protestant

Roman Catholic

Mix (Protestant and Roman Catholic)

ISLAM

HINDUISM

BUDDHISM

CONFUCIANISM/TAOISM

This map is shaded according to the religion practiced
by the majority of the people living in each area. An
absence of shading, such as that in Africa, indicates an
area where none of the major religions predominates.

ASIA

AUSTRALIA

PEOPLE PRACTICING THE SEVEN MAJOR RELIGIONS
Source: World Almanac, 1995

WORLD		NORTH AMERICA	
Judaism	18.1 million	Judaism	6.8 million
Christianity	1.9 billion*	Christianity	241 million*
Eastern Orthodox	*174 million*	*Eastern Orthodox*	*6 million*
Protestant	*383 million*	*Protestant*	*97 million*
Roman Catholic	*1 billion*	*Roman Catholic*	*98 million*
Islam	1 billion	Islam	3.3 million
Hinduism	752 million	Hinduism	1.3 million
Buddhism	335 million	Buddhism	560,000
Confucianism	6.2 million	Confucianism	26,000
Traditional Chinese religions (including Taoism)	141 million	Traditional Chinese religions (including Taoism)	123,000

*The totals given for Christianity include Eastern Orthodox, Protestant, Roman Catholic, Anglican, and other Christians.

TIMELINE OF THE SEVEN MAJOR RELIGIONS

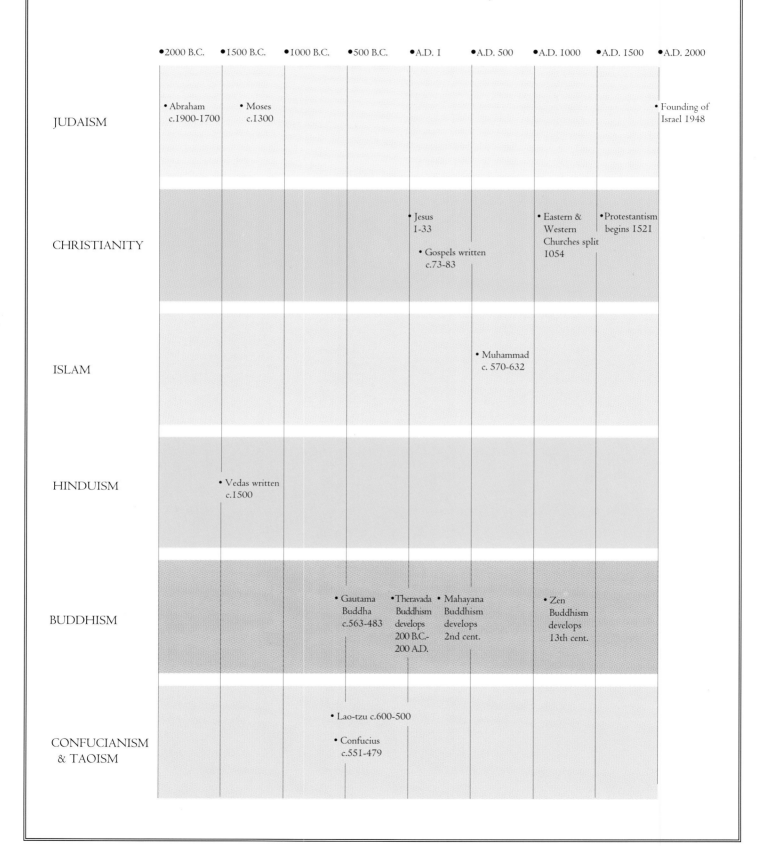

	•2000 B.C.	•1500 B.C.	•1000 B.C.	•500 B.C.	•A.D. 1	•A.D. 500	•A.D. 1000	•A.D. 1500	•A.D. 2000
JUDAISM	• Abraham c.1900-1700	• Moses c.1300							• Founding of Israel 1948
CHRISTIANITY					• Jesus 1-33 • Gospels written c.73-83		• Eastern & Western Churches split 1054	• Protestantism begins 1521	
ISLAM						• Muhammad c. 570-632			
HINDUISM		• Vedas written c.1500							
BUDDHISM				• Gautama Buddha c.563-483	•Theravada Buddhism develops 200 B.C.-200 A.D.	• Mahayana Buddhism develops 2nd cent.	• Zen Buddhism develops 13th cent.		
CONFUCIANISM & TAOISM				• Lao-tzu c.600-500 • Confucius c.551-479					

BIBLIOGRAPHY

Carmody, Denise Lardner, and John Carmody. *The Story of World Religions*. Mountain View, Calif.: Mayfield Publishing Company, 1988.

Chaikin, Miriam. *Menorahs, Mezuzas, and Other Jewish Symbols*. New York: Clarion Books, 1990.

Earhart, H. Byron. *Religions of Japan*. San Francisco: Harper & Row, 1986.

Ellwood, Robert S. *Many Peoples, Many Faiths*. Englewood Cliffs, N.J.: Prentice-Hall, Inc., 1992.

Encyclopedia of World Religions. London: Octopus Books Ltd., 1975.

Fellows, Ward J. *Religions East and West*. New York: Holt, Rinehart and Winston, 1979.

Fisher, Mary Pat, and Robert Luyster. *Living Religions*. Englewood Cliffs, N.J.: Prentice-Hall, Inc., 1991.

Gaer, Joseph. *What the Great Religions Believe*. New York: Dodd, Meade and Co., 1963.

Gordon, Matthew S. *Islam*. New York: Facts on File, 1991.

Hopfe, Lewis M. *Religions of the World*. New York: Macmillan Publishing Co., 1991.

Liston, Robert A. *By These Faiths, Religions for Today*. New York: Julian Messner, 1977.

Mitchell, Stephen. *Tao Te Ching*. New York: HarperCollins, 1988.

Neihardt, John G. *Black Elk Speaks*. Lincoln, Nebr.: University of Nebraska Press, 1979.

Overmyer, Daniel L. *Religions of China*. San Francisco: Harper & Row, 1986.

Parrinder, Geoffrey. *African Mythology*. New York: Peter Bedrick Books, 1987.

Ray, Benjamin C. *African Religions: Symbol, Ritual and Community*. Englewood Cliffs, N.J.: Prentice-Hall, Inc., 1976.

Savage, Katharine. *The Story of World Religions*. New York: Henry Z. Walck, Inc., 1967.

Seeger, Elizabeth. *Eastern Religions*. New York: Thomas Y. Crowell, 1973.

Smith, Huston. *The Religions of Man*. New York: Harper & Row, 1986.

Speight, R. Marston. *God Is One: The Way of Islam*. New York: Friendship Press, 1989.

Waley, Arthur, trans. *The Analects of Confucius*. New York: Vintage Books, 1989.

Weir, Robert F., ed. *The Religious World, Communities of Faith*. New York: Macmillan Publishing Co., 1982.

The World's Great Religions. New York: Time, Inc., 1958.

INDEX

INDEX

INDEX

INDEX

MAKING
EDWARDIAN
COSTUMES
FOR WOMEN